USSR

Marion Sichel

Chelsea House Publishers
New York • New Haven • Philadelphia

© Marion Sichel 1986
First published 1986

Printed in Great Britain

Published in the U.S.A. by Chelsea House Publishers
5014 West Chester Pike, Edgemont, Pa., 19028

Published in the U.K. by B T Batsford Limited
4 Fitzhardinge Street, London W1H 0AH

Library of Congress Cataloging in Publication Data
Sichel, Marion.
   USSR.
   Bibliography: p.
   Summary: Presents in text and illustrations the traditional
costumes of the U.S.S.R. Includes a full description of each
costume, its cultural significance, its historical derivation, and
the context in which the costume was worn.
   1. Costume—Soviet Union.   [1. Costume—Soviet
Union]   I. Title.
GT1040.S53 1986   391'.00947   86-9745
ISBN 1-55546-157-3

A group from various parts of the USSR. The girl on the far left is a Cossack from the Caucasus. The soldier in the front is dancing a typical Russian step crouched down on his heels. The woman, centre back, is in a festive dress from the Ryazan district, whilst on the right is a Turkmen carrying a Bukhara carpet. He is wearing a typical sheepskin headdress rather like a bearskin

CONTENTS

Woman from Yevenki in the Tuva district in skins and ornamental dress RSFSR

On the left the Cheremis woman is dressed in a late nineteenth century costume. The girl in the centre from Latvia is in a present-day folk dress, whilst the one on the right, from Leningrad, is attired in late nineteenth century garb

NORWAY

SWEDEN

FINLAND

BARENTS SEA

ZEMLYA

NOVAYA

Gulf of Bothnia

BALTIC SEA

KARELIA

POLAND

LITHUANIA

LATVIA

ESTONIA

Leningrad

Arkhangel

ARCTIC CIRCLE

BYELO-RUSSIA

MOLDAVIA

UKRAINE

Dnepr

Kiev

Moscow

Kazan

Volga

RUSSIAN SOVIET

Ob

MOUNTAINS

SOCIALIST

Sverdlovsk

BLACK SEA

Don

CAUCASUS

CAUCASUS

GEORGIA

MTS

Stalingrad

URAL

Omsk

Astrakhan

TURKEY

AZER-BAIJAN

ARMENIA

CASPIAN SEA

Baku

ARAL SEA

KAZAKHSTAN

Lake Balkhash

IRAQ

UZBEKISTAN

TURKMENISTAN

IRAN (PERSIA)

Bukhara

Alma-Ata

KIRGHIZIA

TADZHIKISTAN

AFGHANISTAN

0   300   6

4

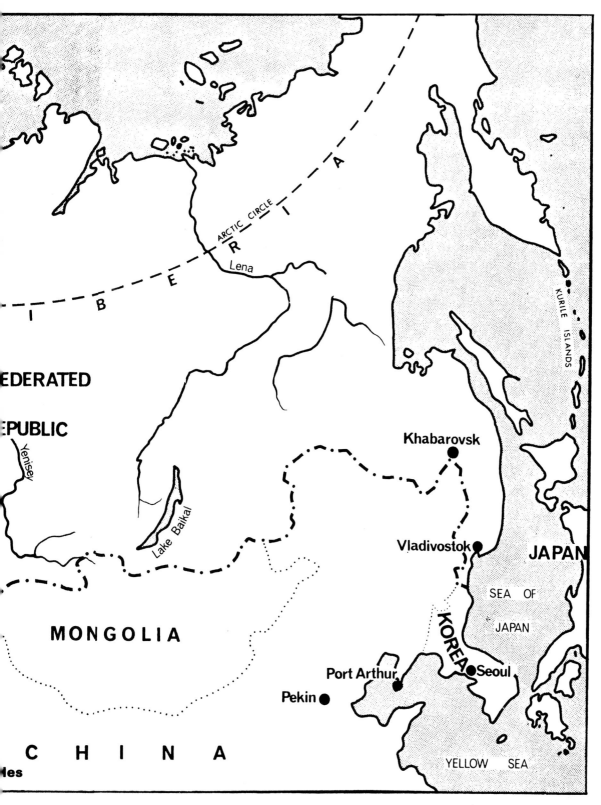

EDERATED

EPUBLIC

Yenisey

ARCTIC CIRCLE

Lena

R
I
B
E
R
I
A

MONGOLIA

Lake Baikal

CHINA

les

Khabarovsk

Vladivostok

JAPAN

SEA OF

JAPAN

KURILE ISLANDS

KOREA

Port Arthur

Seoul

Pekin

YELLOW SEA

300 miles = 483 kilometres
600 miles = 965 kilometres

5

PREFACE

School girl, called a Young Pioneer, wearing a fur cap with earflaps and a Soviet badge

In the vast area of the USSR can be seen many different types of traditional costume showing not only regional differences but also variations of style.

Early in the eighteenth century Czar Peter the Great professed admiration for things European, and western clothing was introduced and worn by those peoples living in towns and centres of industry, but in the rural areas the national and regional dress continued to be worn and retain its original characteristics.

Following the Revolution of 1917, the peasant population too was affected by the western influence and the wearing of national costume is slowly dying out except for weddings and special festivals.

The line drawings in this book are based mainly on photographs of genuine traditional costumes, many of which are in the author's collection. It is hoped that these excellent illustrations will convey the 'flavour' of the many traditional costumes of the USSR and inspire the reader to further study.

Special thanks go to the staff at the Elsie Timbey Collection, and Beryl Graham and Roxane Permar in particular at the Society for Cultural Relations with the USSR who were at all times most co-operative and helpful in providing material.

A troika belonging to a Russian family. The three horses are yoked and guided by four reins, two for the centre horse and one each for the others. Their silver studded harness is adorned with jingling bells, and the high wooden duga borne by the centre horse is decorated with silver stars on a light blue background. The outer horses galloped with their heads turned outwards whilst the centre one trotted rapidly

INTRODUCTION

Coronet shaped headdress of a girl from Latvia. The white blouse is decorated with black embroidery at the top, and the sleeveless bodice has a braid edging matching that of the skirt

A flowered headdress, very popular in Russia

The USSR, the largest country in the world, covers about one sixth of the earth's surface but considering its great size the population is comparatively sparse. However, it is composed of over 100 nationalities speaking some 150 languages and dialects, all united by Socialism and the Communist Party of the Soviet Union, but with each nationality having its own distinctive life style.

The USSR experiences every type of climate from Artic to sub-tropical and every geographical feature is represented from lake and plain to mountain and active volcano. Mineral wealth is widely distributed; there are coal fields and oil fields; forests; fishing along the coasts; horses and cattle bred and reared in the Steppes; cereals grown over vast areas; and plentiful reindeer herds and valuable fur-bearing animals in the north.

For administrative purposes the USSR is divided into 15 Soviet Republics. The Russian Soviet Federative Socialist Republic (RSFSR), in itself a complex ethnic entity, is by far the largest Republic, stretching from its western frontiers in Europe, east to the Pacific Ocean; north to the Arctic Ocean; and south to the frontiers of Mongolia and China.

Whilst Russia is the most eastern nation of Europe, it is also the most western of the orient, thus being influenced by oriental characteristics as well as by western ideas. The lands west of the Ural Mountains are inhabited by three East Slavic peoples; the Russians; the Byelorussians and the Ukrainians. The Cossacks, originally a famous warrior race, still proud of their traditions, live in Caucasia, the mountainous district between the Black Sea and the Caspian Sea, and the Tatars, descendents of the once dreaded Mongols, live on the banks of the River Volga and the land north of the Black Sea.

In the northern areas the women's national dress consists basically of a blouse, a sarafan and an apron. Decorative headwear is also an important accessory, the characteristic being high wide hoops fastened together at the nape of the neck by patterned strips of material.

A *sarafan* is either a skirt or a combined skirt and bodice. With the former a separate sleeveless bodice would be worn. A girdle is tied at one side, the fringed ends of which are sometimes decorated with glass beads and hanging down almost to the hem. For festive wear it is made of brightly coloured silk, brocade or velvet, and decorated with buttons, braids, ribbons and fine metal chains. For everyday wear it is of handwoven fabric – often black – the top being embroidered with coloured wools.

Under the sarafan is worn a white muslin blouse. For everyday wear there is little ornamentation but for festive occasions the collar, front and sleeves of the blouse, then made of linen or silk, are richly embroidered by hand. The designs vary in different regions but are mostly rosette variations or stylised birds. The embroidery on the skirts incorporates birds, horses, trees and human figures. These designs date back to antiquity, probably reflecting the pagan ideas of the forces of nature, and the general life styles of the peoples.

A *vorotushka* a shirt-blouse of fine linen with red weft threads, was introduced from the Arkhangel district and worn on special occasions when young girls, too, are permitted to wear a belted blouse, known as a *pokosnitsa*, with an ornamented skirt.

In many areas long aprons are worn, richly embroidered, the tops in light colours, graduating to darker colouring at the hem.

The men dress in embroidered cotton shirts with their trousers tucked into their leather knee-length boots. In winter special felt boots are worn as well as heavy sheepskin coats and hats.

Being workers on the land their girdles often have special pockets attached to hold such items as seeds. For festive wear the ends of the girdles are plaited and finished with tassels embellished with beads.

The festive dress includes a *paneka* or *korotenka*, the names given to short dresses similar to the sarafan. When opened out this style forms a circle of fabric. In the late seventeenth century these dresses were made of flowered patterned silk and ornamented with braids, but in the early nineteenth century they were of brocade, heavily embroidered with gold thread, and gathered at the back in tubular folds. The korotenka has survived in the Mezen district of the Arkhangel province, being now worn mainly at folk festivals. Padded jackets of red damask and velvet, with long sleeves and waisted with tubular folds, are also characteristic of the northern areas.

Northern Russian woman wearing a sheepskin coat or tulup with a sash around the waist

Child's apron as seen in European Russia

Russian peasant woman with an apron and headscarf ready to go to market with her piglet

In the southern areas the *ponyova*, a thigh-length skirt, is worn over a blouse, attached around the waist with a braided cord. Such skirts are usually made of dark blue or black woollen fabric and embroidered or decorated with lacework or braids. The embroidery on the blouse is of geometrical design differentiating it from the figurative work of the north. Ribbons and braids are used extensively, often completely covering the shoulders and sleeves. A straight apron, sometimes with sleeves, is worn over the blouse and skirt, and this is also richly embroidered.

A *naverschnik*, an ancient type of tunic, often black, is worn as an over-garment. The headdress is usually most decorative, the forms of ornamentation being very varied. There is also a distinction between the headdress of married women and that of single girls. Married women, according to the eastern Slav traditions, have to cover their hair, usually with an elegant cap, whilst young girls may plait their hair and go about bareheaded or wear a kerchief or hoop-like headdress which reveals their hair.

One of the most common styles is a *kokoshnik*, a cap embroidered with pearls, and gold thread on a mother-of-pearl mesh, hanging over the brow. In the central regions *kokoshniki* are high crowned and in some areas they are in the form of a crescent or triangle. One elegant style has a tall peak studded with rubies and other precious stones, but tall felt-topped hats with narrow brims and bands of twisted cord around the crown are more generally worn.

Young girls' headdresses also vary in form, usually consisting of a narrow crown decorated with silk, beads and feathers or balls of goose down. Complicated headdresses, known as *soroka*, are also popular. These are trimmed with contrasting multi-coloured glass beads, gold thread, feathers and fringes.

Men's attire is more uniform and almost always consists of coarse linen shirts with side fastenings and striped handwoven trousers. The hats and caps are usually made of felt from sheeps' wool.

In cold weather both men and women wear raw sheepskin coats covered with a blue printed fabric.

Lapti made of fibres from birch and lime trees are the most common type of shoe worn in summer in rural areas. These are attached to the feet by long strings known as *obory* and wound around the legs over a white fabric. For festive occasions leather boots are worn.

The women also wear leather shoes called *khoty*, trimmed

Woman from Great Russia wearing a girdled sarafan with shoulder straps over a blouse-like shirt. The headdress, a kokoshnik, *worn with a veil*

with nails. Felt boots or *valenki* are worn in the winter.

To the east there still remain a few pure Mongols and Tatars who have preserved their own characteristics and continue to lead a nomadic life, their everyday dress being adapted to the climatic conditions. Most of their clothing is quilted to provide warmth during the cold winter months.

The Chinese influence can be seen in the women's elaborate hairstyles and costumes which are worn on special occasions. They consist of long coats with padded shoulders, extremely long sleeves with large cuffs and exotic winged or conical headwear which is richly encrusted with jewels and precious metals.

The Slavs who inhabit the central and southern regions are known as *Ukrainians*, whilst the *Russians* are a mixture of Slav and Finn with Tatar influence becoming dominant after the Mongol invasion in the thirteenth century.

To the west of the Urals lies European Russia including the Baltic Republics of Estonia, Latvia and Lithuania, large areas of which are given over to agriculture and cattle breeding. The national dress is markedly more subdued than that of other regions, with a predominence of greyish colours.

The merchants always wore distinctive costume; a type of frock coat, tight around the neck, trousers tucked into high boots, and a peaked cap. Their beards were long and their hair cut straight across at the back of the neck.

The many different types of costume seen in the vast area of the USSR show regional differences and variations of style, also characteristic details of pattern, design and colour of the embroideries and headdress which distinguish the costume of one district or village from that of another. The richness of the embroidery seen throughout the country is recognised as an important part of the cultural heritage of the USSR.

A muzhik or peasant dressed in an old military style winter sheepskin coat and an astrakhan cap. The trousers are tucked into the high boots

Ornamental wooden shoe with a leather strap worn with many of the folk costumes

10

The woman from the Kolga-Jaani area is wearing a characteristically wide collar and a large round brooch. The bodice is of a dark blue colour. The coif is stiffly starched and resembles a cock's tail

BALTIC REPUBLICS

Estonia, Latvia and Lithuania all lie on the south-east coast of the Baltic Sea, Estonia being the most northern, with Latvia in the centre, and Lithuania the most southerly; agriculture and cattle breeding being the main way of life. They have close links with Western Europe and Roman Catholicism, and have basically similar dress.

Before modernisation of the roads skirts were worn very short in the winter because of the high snow drifts through which the people had to walk. Due to the long cold winters most country people wear high felt boots called *valenki*, in preference to leather ones, although these could not be worn in wet weather as they would have become soaking wet. These boots are similar to those worn throughout the country.

In common with many other northern territories, stripes prevail. The skirts made of heavy material are gathered in small tucks on to a waist band, dark red being the predominant colour although black, yellow and orange were also popular. The belts often have loose pockets attached. The white, long-sleeved blouses have lace edged collars fastened with a brooch. Sleeveless jackets, when worn, are usually fastened with silver rosettes. The stockings usually white, may also be striped or patterned and the shoes, usually black, have decorated tongues.

Men wear long sleeved white shirts fastened at the neck with a brooch or braided tie; their black breeches fastenedd at the knees with silver buckles. A patterned or dark waistcoat was also worn as well as a braided belt, and a high felt hat.

A woman's red and black tasselled ► cap from the island of Kihelkonna

Estonian peasant costume. High felt top hat and long white sleeved, high necked shirt with a cord around the waist

Peasants as dressed in the early part of the twentieth century. The girl in the centre is from the Moscow district and the man on the right is a Tatar – a community that is widespread in Russia

ESTONIA

Estonia is separated from Finland by the Gulf of Finland and, from about the fifth century, has been inhabited by people of Finnish descent.

Estonian folk costume was influenced by neighbouring countries and ideas adapted according to their taste. Estonia can be divided into several regional groups, the main ones being to the north, south and west as well as the islands. The costumes have several features common with those of Lithuania and Latvia, such as tunic-like shirt, but without shoulder seams, an oblong wrap worn over the shoulders and a wrap-around skirt. Striped materials are common to all three Baltic States.

A distinctive part of Estonian national dress is a large *plastron* of finely chased and embossed silver, as well as silver trinkets sewn on the sleeveless bodice. A mitre shaped headdress also forms part of the national costume. The remainder of the dress is relatively simple but rich in embroidery.

Young girls wear decorated headbands or garlands of flowers, whilst married women are required to cover their heads.

From the seventeenth century men from the northern parts of Estonia started to wear chamois leather breeches, more like those worn in Scandinavia and Central Europe, whilst the women began to embroider their skirt hemlines with coloured beads.

Previously linen kerchiefs were worn as headwear, but from then onwards small coifs became more fashionable, and shoes and boots were also introduced.

In the eighteenth century the narrower skirts were replaced by fuller ones, first in plain colours, but later in vertical stripes. Green woollen aprons with red wool bands and gilt thread decoration also became more popular, homespun materials being replaced by manufactured fabrics. A necklace of glass beads completed the costume.

In some areas silk caps made on cardboard frames were worn, and floral patterned embroidery was also seen.

Towards the end of the nineteenth century, the local differences in dress became less apparent, and by the twentieth century folk costumes were worn mainly at national festivals and on special occasions.

A complete festive costume is given to a young adult on confirmation.

Traditional mourning attire from Jamaja. Over the underskirt, a short white blouse with a buttoned collar is worn. The dark pleated skirt is sewn to the bodice. The apron, tasselled cap and the belt are in darker colours for mourning

A long coat worn by men and women alike in Southern Estonia. It is waisted with gores

*Typical of Hargla, the shirts have
turned-down collars embroidered
with geometrical patterns. The
woollen jacket is ornamented with
red and green cord. The coat is of thin
white cotton with a wide lace
trimming. She is also wearing a
conical brooch*

*The married woman from the Setu
region wearing a long white woollen
winter coat. A kerchief is folded back
at the corners over her headwear, in
this case a veil. Ornaments are worn
over the overcoat*

*In the background the two Estonian peasant women
are wearing large sheepskin coats with the fleece on
the inside. They also wear thick boots to keep out the
severe cold of the winter. They are sawing logs, this
being one of the main sources of fuel. The young girl
on the left is in a colourful national costume. The
sleeveless bodice is fastened with silver rosettes. Her
skirt is in the popular striped material. The Estonian
fisherman is playing a crude musical instrument,
reminiscent of a Scottish bagpipe*

*Young Estonian girl wearing
mitre-shaped ornamented headwear
as part of her national costume*

13

A typical bridal dress from Oesel Island in Estonia is brightly coloured and heavily embroidered; red being the dominant colour. The hat, a most important feature, is covered in hanging glass balls and clusters of feathers.

A typical Estonian peasant wedding costume from the island of Dago consists of a pleated striped skirt and a short sleeved blouse worn over a double-breasted calico bodice, and broad leather girdle with chain ornamentation hanging at the back. A narrow cloak, which covers only the back, may be worn for these occasions, made of light material, and coloured silk bands with beaded designs hanging from it. A rose wreath around the head, or a hat in red calico heavily ornamented with glass beads, is also part of the wedding outfit.

White used to be the colour for mourning, without any decorations, but from the middle of the nineteenth century on the islands of Saaremaa and Hiiumaa and in western Estonia, dark colours were introduced, but never any red. Headwear was embroidered in black or white and without streamers.

LATVIA

Latvia borders on to the Baltic Sea. They are a people of indeterminable origin, close to the Hungarians, and speaking their own highly developed language.

The old time costumes have almost disappeared, but in some remoter districts the picturesque attire of the past can still be seen on festive occasions.

The national dress is simple and attractive. Generally a wide sleeved embroidered blouse with a red and yellow apron of a geometrical design, a full blue skirt and a long fringed headscarf. For warmth, a sheepskin coat with the wool on the inside is also worn, lavishly embroidered for special occasions. Footwear consists of *pastali*, which are hide sandals.

There are many variations of the basic costume, one such, worn by women, has a long full dark coloured skirt with a deep red patterned border. The long loose-sleeved blouse is decorated with black embroidery round the neck, on the outer sides of the sleeves and on the shoulders. The sleeveless bodice in red, matching the border of the skirt, is ornamented with silver braid. Coronet shaped headdresses and richly embossed breast buckles are a main feature of the full traditional attire.

The men wear calf-length light coloured coats embroidered in black down the front edge. The light coloured trousers are

This simple handwoven Latvian national costume is worn with a type of shawl fastened on the shoulder with a popular fibula *brooch. The long loose sleeved blouse is decorated at the wrist and turned-down collar. The headdress consists of a crown shaped embroidered hat*

Fibula with an ornate design worn on the shoulder of a Latvian costume

14

Old Latvian traditional folk costume with richly embossed breast buckles and an imposing coronet-shaped headdress

gathered on to a band around the ankles and the white shirt, with its turned down collar, has a knotted bow at the neck. A long braid belt is tied around the coat. Most embroidery and braid is red.

'What is red is beautiful' is an old Latvian proverb and until the middle of the nineteenth century an entirely red costume was worn in the northern area.

In the Pernau region of Latvia a man's sleeveless sheepskin coat is trimmed and ornamented with patent leather appliqué, the high stand-up collar is lined with fur. This type of coat has been common in Russia for centuries and is often worn with long sleeves, with the front seam left open so that the arms can protrude, leaving the sleeves either hanging loosely or knotted together at the back.

A woman's overcoat from the same region is often made of a felt – similar to woollen twill – with only the collar lined with calico. Trimmings of red cord and gold braid on the side slits are a very popular form of decoration.

The country people, on special feast days, apart from wearing their traditional costumes, decorate themselves with garlands of foliage, mainly of oak leaves.

A Latvian couple in their traditional country costume. The woman's headscarf is colourful adding brightness to the otherwise plain attire. The legs are thickened by wearing several pairs of stockings over each other

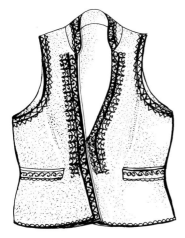

The sleeveless vest has a braided geometrical design around the edges and is worn with the Latvian costume

LITHUANIA

Lithuania is wedged between Latvia, Byelorussia and Poland. The Lithuanians are one of the most ancient peoples in Europe, a blonde, blue-eyed race, tall and strong. Many Lithuanian costumes are basically similar to those in the other Baltic Republics; women wearing blouses, skirts and aprons, and men wearing shirts, trousers and waistcoats.

White is worn for all important Church festivals, always richly embroidered. Coloured dress is more fashionable for everyday wear. In common with many other countries, few of the traditional features of the national dress survive. Characteristic of women's dress is a full-length wide robe of linen or wool which envelopes the entire figure. It is fastened at the shoulder by a large round silver clasp ornamented with floral designs in relief. Their headdresses consist of circlets with streamers or veils hanging loosely at the back.

Typical Lithuanian headdress

The oldest traditional women's costume consists of a namitka, a laced corset with metal fastenings, a skirt, a long dark blue coat and a linen apron with an embroidered band at the hem, now worn only on special occasions.

A *namitka*, still worn to day, is made of lengths of white linen which are wound around the head and neck the ends hanging loose down the back or over the shoulders.

The coat in recent years has become shorter reaching only to the knees, closely pleated from the bust down, known as a *simtakvaldis*, meaning 'a hundred pleats'.

A long handwoven woollen coat of dark blue or grey is worn by the men, similar in style to that worn by the women.

In the north the fur cap is still in evidence. Plaited leather shoes are for general use and wooden shoes, called *klumpes*, with carved or painted ornamentation are also worn.

Typical Lithuanian plaid designed material often seen in the Aukstaciai region

A bridal costume of the north differs from that of other regions with its distinctive headdress made of coloured ribbons.

To the southern and eastern boundaries woollen girdles are extremely popular, ornamented at either end with fringes.

The variation in men's costume is mainly in colour and woven patterns, whilst the women's differed in the cut of the bodice, the embroidered design on the chemise and apron as well as the colours used, also the style of and decoration on the headdress.

In the Vilnius district, covering numerous villages, each with its own variations, a girl may wear a fitted yellow bodice patterned in red and green, whilst the skirt would be yellow

A profusely embroidered geometrical design at the cuff to which the sleeve is gathered

16

with mauve, orange and black designs. The veil, chemise and apron would be white with red and blue geometric designs.

In the Klaipeda district the skirt is predominantly blue with thin red stripes, and red geometric designs on the chemise and apron. A blue veil is embroidered in white and the collar and bodice edged with white ruffles.

Yet in another region, the Aukstaciai, the colours are predominantly green with yellow, brown and red plaid designs. The pointed bodice, chemise, and apron patterned in green and red are handwoven and sometimes embroidered.

Some of the most charming of the Lithuanian folk dance costumes are in various shades of blue. The long handwoven skirts with horizontal bands and stripes are worn with sleeveless hip length jackets, also striped. The aprons vary in design and colour; white with blue embroidery and a white fringe or of a blue and red pattern on a light blue background with a red fringe. The full sleeved white blouse has a small turned-down collar, the lower part of the sleeves, cuffs and collar, as well as the front have blue embroidery. The headwear consists of a small decorated crown. The shoes in white or blue have cross-over straps around the ankles.

The men also wear light blue outfit. The sleeveless jacket is worn over a long sleeved white shirt with embroidery at the cuffs and a braided knotted tie. The jacket fastens at the waist with two buttons, the edges decorated with braiding. The coloured braid belt with fringed ends is worn under the jacket. The shoes are similar in style to those of the women.

High laced boot worn in the early part of the twentieth century

Detail of a sleeve of a blouse with ▶ the main embroidery just above the cuff

Lithuanian costumes basically similar to those of the other Baltic States

Lithuanian costumes basically similar to those of the other Baltic States

Back and front view of an early type of Lithuanian national dress. Plain and striped skirts were worn with striped aprons. The sleeveless waistcoats were often ruched just below the bosom and could be of plaid or plain materials with bands of decorative designs. Short shawl-like scarves are worn over the shoulders, and headscarves could be tied on the top, giving a turban-like appearance. Favourite colours for these clothes are reds, blues and white

Front and back view of a Lithuanian dress. The handwoven skirt had horizontal bands of colour and the sleeveless hip-length jacket striped vertically, are worn over a white blouse. The headwear is a stiffened band with streamers behind

18

BYELORUSSIA

Young woman in a traditional bridal costume from Radostovo in the Drogichin region

The word 'Byelorussia' means White Russia, so called because of the local dress of white flax worn by the inhabitants. Bounded on the west by Poland and on the south by the Ukraine, it is a country of dense forests, innumerable lakes, rivers and marshes. The Byelorussians, of Slavonic descent, are generally brown eyed and brown haired. Even today the traditional folk costumes and folklore play an important part in the life of the people.

The sarafan is more bell-shaped than that in other regions, with straps over the shoulders. The upper part is made of calico and faced with linen edged with a contrasting colour, whilst the skirt, also of calico, has a printed check design with wide braided borders. Over the sarafan an apron, similar to a skirt, but left open on one side, is fastened with a drawstring or button at the yoke. Married women wear a bonnet or a *nuometas*, while young girls wear coronet style headdresses or narrow headscarves.

Men's costume includes long linen shirts worn over tight trousers, and in certain regions, a waistcoat and a leather bag. Several styles of caps, and straw hats, are worn in summer. In winter they wear sheepskin hats with earflaps.

Warm overcoats of grey or white woollen fabric, known as *sviti*, are worn by both men and women, as are white or red-ochre sheepskin coats or jackets.

Footwear consists of leather shoes for winter and lapti for summer.

A women's costume worn for national dancing consists of a full skirt in a plaid material, an apron and a white linen full-sleeved blouse with frilled cuffs. The blouse, like the apron, is embroidered in a red geometrical design. A sleeveless jacket is fastened either by lacing or buttoning. Several white petticoats are worn beneath the skirt. The waist band varies in colour and ornamentation according to the region. A long embroidered white scarf is tied around the head with the ends hanging down at the back. Their ankle boots are laced.

Traditional summer wear for a man from Zbliany in the Lida district

Over loose baggy striped trousers that are tucked into black or brown leather boots, the men wear full sleeved white shirts with the stand-up collar, the front panels and cuffs embroidered with a red geometrical design.

Young man from Zbliany in the Lida district in a traditional summer folk costume showing the embroidery

Early twentieth century festive ▶ *costume from Tyshkovichi in the region of Ivanovo*

Festive costume, early twentieth century, from Chersk in the Brest region

A matchmaker's costume from Povitye in the Kobrin area

Costume of a man from the Mogilev area. Over the linen trousers and shirt he wears a buttonless coat with a stand-up collar, the karakin. In winter the coat is of wool and in summer of natural coloured linen. The bast shoes are held on by cord or thonging

UKRAINE

Young Ukrainian girl with a turban-like kerchief and several necklaces worn over a high-necked chemise with the full embroidered sleeves. The corset-like bodice worn over this has a scalloped base

Ukrainian man wearing a hat decorated for festival wear, with feathers and flowers

The Ukraine occupies the southern part of the Great Russian plain bordering the Black Sea enjoying a comparatively mild climate and some of the best arable soil in Eastern Europe.

The Ukrainians are pure Slavs and the true descendants of the founders of Russia. Kiev, the capital, is both the cradle of the Slav nation and of Christianity which played such a prominent part in the later stages of Slav history. The Ukrainians retain their strong sense of national identity and are famous for their national songs and dances.

The national costume for both men and women is characterised by rich embroidery with distinctive variations of style from district to district. In the northern region the most primitive embroideries prevail marked by geometrical designs almost exclusively in red. In the province of Poltava, in Central Ukraine, the dark coloured dresses are relieved only by white embroidered sleeves.

The costumes of the majority of peasant women are generally very simple, the main garment being a chemise, with embroidery around the neck and down the front opening, as well as on the sleeves which are gathered at the wrists. Over the chemise is worn an apron, open at one side and held in place with a sash. A turban-like kerchief and necklaces complete the outfit. For more festive occasions the designs are similar but the materials used are of a finer quality and the embroidery richer and more colourful. A sleeveless 'smock' made of dark plaid fabric is worn over the outfit and edged with contrasting colours. High boots are worn, or *chereviki*, which are shoes made of coloured leather. A crown headdress with garlands of flowers and coloured flowing ribbons are also part of the festive costume.

Young girls wear embroidered chemises with full short sleeves, and a bright plaid skirt open in the front and covered by a brightly coloured or embroidered apron.

A contemporary festival costume consists of a white linen chemise and a coloured skirt, both lavishly embroidered in floral designs. The black woollen handwoven apron is profusely embroidered in a multitude of colours, and has a sash of black and white checked cotton, edged with black. The high boots are of red leather.

Another contemporary festive costume consists of a white linen smock with red, green and yellow embroidery on the hem and sleeves. A red and green silk sash is tied around the waist. The sleeveless jacket is of white linen edged with black lambs' wool and embroidered in black.

For performing their traditional dances the women's costume has a unique style. A short woollen brightly coloured skirt is worn over a slightly longer petticoat, with a white embroidered apron over the skirt, hiding the front opening. The white blouse is embroidered in a floral design down the front and on the full sleeves. A dark wool or velvet sleeveless jacket fastening on the left side is embroidered around the edges and worn over the blouse. The floral headdress, with streamers of coloured ribbons hanging at the back, remain ever fashionable as do the red leather boots.

The men's costume is simpler than that of the women, consisting of a white shirt with wide sleeves, embroidered on the collar, down the front opening and round the cuffs, and full white linen trousers, tucked into high top boots usually of red leather. A sash is worn around the waist, the ends hanging one on each side.

A type of overcoat, called a *svita*, is worn by both men and women. It is of white grey or brown homespun cloth; tight at the waist and trimmed with coloured cords. An astrakhan cap is worn in the winter.

Milk sellers used to be familiar figures in Kiev and wore picturesque costumes, the girls wearing top boots and long quilted petticoats or printed cottons with embroidered aprons and coloured headscarves.

Festive costume of finer material than for ordinary wear. The apron is brightly coloured. The sleeveless smock widens at the back with an edging of contrasting colour. The high boots are an essential part of the costume and the headwear, a kind of crown or diadem, has colourful paper flowers attached

Far right
Typical Ukrainian costume with the tops of the sleeves embroidered and a turban-like headdress with tassels

Ukrainian girl wearing a fringed headscarf

Ukrainian girl in an embroidered full sleeved chemise. The embroidered headdress has a pompon decoration either side

The shirt of this man from the Chernigov district is embroidered down the front and cuffs

The woman on the left is dressed in the older style of folk costume of the Poltavo district, with a turban-like headdress and necklaces. The apron is held on with a sash. The girl on the right, from the Kiev region, has long plaited hair. The loose sleeveless jacket is trimmed wtih pink and black braid. Over the long skirt, from beneath which can just be seen the petticoat, is covered in front with a black apron. The man, also from the Kiev region, is wearing a straw hat, embroidered open-necked shirt and baggy trousers tucked into high boots with a broad girdle around the waist

Young Ukrainian girl with a headscarf tied at the back. The high-necked blouse is profusely embroidered on the top part of the sleeves

A young Ukrainian in a minus hat and a sleeveless sheepskin jacket profusely embroidered. Beneath this is worn a long shirt with the sleeves gathered at the wrists

Costumes from the Volyn region in the Ukraine. The front and back view of the woman shows the flowered headscarf, and the short basqued jacket embroidered around the edges and at the back. Over the red and yellow striped skirt she wears an apron. The man in his twentieth century costume is wearing a tall astrakhan cap and well below the knee length coat with broad trimmings, and a sash around the waist

Woman of the Stanislav district wearing an ornate necklace made of coins

24

The summer dress of a Ukrainian man from the Chernovtsy province ►

Red festival cap with gold thread embroidery from the Tadzhik area

Ukrainian boy in a wide brimmed straw hat. The loose jacket is decorated with frogging, ending in pompons. Beneath can just be seen the shirt with embroidery around the neck edge and front opening

Woman from the Kiev district wearing a simple costume; a chemise with the sleeves embroidered near the top and gathered at the wrists, also an apron, and a kerchief on her head ◄

Typical Ukrainian in a minus cap and lumber-type jacket with a shirt beneath buttoning down the centre front

One style of dance costume from the Ukraine

The simple peasant costume is
similar to the Walachian or
Podolian. The main garment is a
long chemise in a Slavic design with
the sleeves gathered at the wrists, and
embroidery along all edges. Over the
chemise the apron is worn open on
one side. The fabric belt holds the
apron on. A colourful kerchief is
worn like a turban

Young Ukrainian girl wearing a festive costume
consisting of a skirt, white apron, blouse and
sleeveless jacket, all hand embroidered. The jacket
has bands of embroidery and braid around the edges,
and the white blouse with the three-quarter length
sleeves has a floral embroidered design. The floral
headwear has long ribbon streamers behind, and
several rows of beads adorn her neck. The red boots
complete the outfit. In the background can be sen a
typical milk seller of Kiev, wearing a quilted coat,
the loose trousers tucked into his boots.

Girl from Irkutsk in Siberia in a white blouse,
flowered skirt and dark bibbed apron. She is
wearing strings of beads and a colourful headscarf
tied under her chin

26

Trans-Carpathian young betrothed girl from Isa in a festive headdress, early twentieth century

Ukrainian man wearing a typical soft fur cap ▶

Young man wearing festival apparel, the coat is embroidered with braid. This costume is from the Podolye region

Ukrainian contemporary festive costumes from the Ternopol region. The girl on the left is wearing her petticoat slightly longer than her skirt

MOLDAVIA

Lying to the south of the Ukraine, the Moldavian Soviet Socialist Republic, founded in 1940, is the smallest of the republics.

There are many variations to the folk costumes worn by these peoples who are mainly of Slav origin. Over several layers of petticoats, the women's full pleated skirts are of red, white or black fabric depending on the area, all with deep embroidered hems. An apron, called a *plakha*, covers both front and back, and is woven in brightly coloured horizontal stripes or in a geometric pattern. The long sleeved white linen blouse is heavily embroidered down the sleeves and front. The short sleeved bolero jackets are also profusely embroidered around the edges; beads sometimes being added for further decoration. A red or white kerchief is often worn on the head instead of flowers. Footwear consists of red or black boots, or low heeled shoes.

Men's costumes consist of white embroidered long sleeved shirts with a sash or broad leather belt. Leather sleeveless jackets and astrakhan hats are also worn.

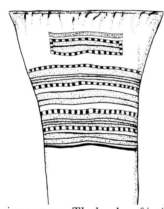

Moldavian costume. The headscarf is tied behind and the sleeveless jacket is embroidered down the front (detail shown). The long white blouse sleeves are embroidered near the top (detail shown)

Typical Moldavian costumes with the striped aprons. The girl on the right is wearing boots and both girls are wearing headscarves. The man in the background is an agricultural worker

The young man on the right is a Moldavian and his jacket is trimmed with astrakhan

RSFSR

The RSFSR covers about three-quarters of the USSR and holds over half the population who, like Byelorussia and the Ukraine, are Slavs with a common cultural background. All these regions have brightly embroidered designs on both the men's and women's dress, especially the shirts and blouses, nearly every district and village having its own special dress. The materials from which the costumes are made are usually woven locally.

Women's indoor dress consists chiefly of the *ponyova* which is a skirt of thick woollen check material, a sarafan, a wide apron with or without sleeves, generally of linen and lavishly embroidered.

The safaran is made of either brocade or a plain material in red, blue or gold. Braid is sewn down the front, along the top of the bodice and at the hem. The round-necked white blouse, worn beneath the sarafan, has full sleeves, either three-quarter length or long, is usually embroidered.

Out of doors women wear fur capes in winter – in summer short coats, or capes made of plain cloth, damask or cloth of gold.

Women's headdresses are the most striking of Russia's traditional costume, reflecting ancient customs. The shape, material and design varying from area to area. There are two basic styles – a headband and a close fitting cap. Young girls wear crowns or diadems revealing their hair at the back, loose or in a single plait, whilst married women are required to cover their hair completely.

The variations of headdresses in the form of crowns and diadems are known as *kokoshnik*, *kichka*, *povoynik*, and *karuna*, all of which are of cloth of gold, damask or velvet and lavishly embroidered with pearls, beads and semi-precious stones.

The *kokoshnik* has a large bow at the back and is profusely decorated with precious jewels. Ornamented headwear is handed down in families from generation to generation.

Over their headdress they have a long wide veil, called a *dymka* or *fata*, which falls partly over the face and is made of white muslin, interwoven with floral designs in silk, or

Lady in eighteenth century traditional dress, from Arkhangel. The sarafan is in a rich material and the sleeves are elaborately embroidered. The magnificent headdress is decorated with precious metals and stones

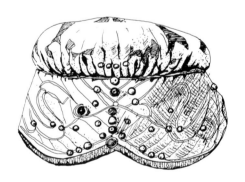

Late nineteenth century headdress, known as a povoynik *from the Vologda province*

An end of eighteenth century basic costume of a Russian woman. This consisted of a chemise, a sarafan and a korotenka worn on top. This style is bell-shaped. The headdress, a kokoshnik is decorated and trimmed with braid

Woman's horned headdress, known as a kichka, *from the Ryazan province, nineteenth century*

embroidered in gold. Sometimes the veil is made in heavy silk, embroidered in gold or decorated with lace and a gold fringe. In some villages they are made of linen embroidered at the edges.

In many districts woollen waistbands, handwoven in a variety of colours, are fastened with dried chicken bones. They also wear chains of filigree work, rings and earrings.

Men generally wear loose shirts over the trousers, with a cord around the waist. The full sleeves are gathered onto embroidered cuffs, with a matching band of embroidery around the high stand-up collar and down the front side opening as well as on the hem. The full black trousers are tucked into black leather boots.

Men's costumes for winter wear is duller and more uniform than the women's, consisting of a kaftan of which there are many variations, capes of fur or sheepskin (the fur worn inside and the skin outside). They also wear tall felt hats or round fur bonnets or caps. Indoors they wear linen trousers, printed by hand or of homespun cloth; shirts either coloured or of white linen embroidered at the edge as well as on the sleeves and collar.

In addition to leather or felt boots, *lapti*, a summer form of footwear made from tree fibre, are common.

Siberia covers the entire northern part of Asia and is bordered on the north by the Artic Ocean on the east by the Bering Sea and the Sea of Okhotsk, on the south by China and on the west by European Russia from which it is divided by the Ural mountains.

Apart from being inhabited by a large number of Russian exiles and their descendants, it is also inhabited by indigenous tribes of Mongolian origin including the Samoyedes, Ostyaks, Voguls, Mongols, Kalmuks, Buryats and Tatars.

The Siberians are a hardy race and of them the Samoyedes – short of stature – are true nomads. They live within the Artic Circle in reindeer-skin tents, and are carried on the backs of their herds as they seek new grazing lands. In the north of Siberia the Chukchis are one of the few peoples who have remained independant. Both men and women dress alike in suits made of seal, walrus and reindeer skins which they hunt and spear. Their chief occupation is preparing seal and walrus hides. The women chew the tough skins for hours, this wears down their teeth to the gums. The Buryats are one of the most numerous races of Siberia.

The Siberian Tatars of whom about two-thirds are of Turkic stock and the remainder of mixed Finnic blood, live mainly

31

north of Lake Baikal.

The Giliaks, from eastern Siberia, are diminutive of stature, the men and women dressing very much alike, although the women's costume is sometimes distinguished by a fringe of metal discs around the hem of the outer garment.

The Yakuts, also of eastern Siberia – of Turkic origin – are shrewd and enterprising. In southern Siberia the Kalmuks who live in the Altai region where the finest forests are to be found, wear their hair in short pigtails. They live in semi-circular felt tents.

The Tungus are hunters and fur traders in the Siberian forest regions. They use reindeer for riding and also for transport. Their national dress has a great Japanese influence.

In the Arkhangel district the national costume of the women consists of a sarafan with a quilted jacket called a *shugais*. These have long elaborate sleeves decorated with embroidery and pearls or braid. Some styles allowed for the long sleeves to fall over the hand in folds.

In the winter a fur jacket is also worn. This is often made of silk brocade and lined with ermine, lambskin being used for the collar and sleeve linings.

The sarafan varies in different regions, those of the northern area are often made of stiff brocades to make the skirts flare out. The tall headdresses are in various shapes, decorated with precious metals and stones, usually worn over a small skull cap.

Men's tunics customarily fasten to the left side in front and have a narrow girdle around the waist. Their trousers are made of hand-printed material. Shoes for summer wear are made of birch bark, but in winter special felt boots are worn.

In the long and cold winters, caps and fur coats, with the fleece on the inside, are needed, sometimes with another heavy woollen coat on top.

At the end of the eighteenth century and the first half of the nineteenth, the most prominent item of dress in the north was a flowered or black sarafan.

The chemise was usually of white linen or muslin, or silk for festival wear, and the skirt in a similar material, or of velvet or brocade and decorated with buttons, braid and multi-coloured ribbons. The top of the chemise and sleeves, which are not covered by the sarafan, are of superior material to that part which is hidden beneath the sarafan. The headdress is either rectangular or half-moon in front decorated with strings of beads, pearls and braid, fastened at the back with wide ribbons. As in other regions a young girl is allowed to show her plaited

Reindeer herder from Nenets, near Arkhangel, wearing a sheepskin coat decorated with a band of appliqué

Yakut woman in a fur coat with bead decoration and astrakhan hat and decorated boots

PLATE 1   The Estonian woman, on the left, from Kihelkonna, is wearing a long sleeved collarless shirt under a short sleeveless bodice that is fastened with three small brooches. Over the pleated striped skirt her white cotton apron is decorated with lace and silk ribbon bands. A separate pocket, profusely decorated with beads, is hooked on to a wide belt. The red and black knitted cap has a long tail with a tassel hanging behind. Her woollen stockings are also red. Her black shoes are tied with a ribbon bow. The little Estonian girl in the foreground, from Jämaja, wears a similar costume to an adult, with the exception of an apron and jacket. She is seen here wearing a knitted tasselled cap. The white blouse has a high collar and very full sleeves gathered at the wrists. The pleated skirt is attached to the sleeveless bodice and the material is in bold horizontal stripes.

The shoes and woollen stockings are black. The girl on the right, from Mormovichi in the Svetlogorsk district of Byelorussia, is in a festive costume. Over her white embroidered long sleeved blouse she is wearing a sleeveless black embroidered bodice with a short basque. Her white apron and her headdress are both embroidered in a red geometric design. The man, in a bridegroom's outfit, is from the Semipalatinsk province of Kazakhstan. His ornate hat has button and woollen tuft decoration. His long, collarless white Cossack type blouse is profusely embroidered and has red calico embroidered trimmings. He wears a long woollen sash around his waist, and his trousers are also embroidered. Over his white ribbed woollen long stockings he wears lapti held on with obory or thonging

PLATE 2   Centre top is an example of fine Kazakh jewellery, three rings attached to a purse, from the Guryev district by the Caspian Sea. In the centre front the older man's costume, from the Alma-ata district bordering on to China, consists of a cap trimmed with fox fur. The coat is of sheepskin surrounded with a jewelled and buckled belt of leather. The woman on the left is from the Akybinsk district which is towards the Aral Sea. She is wearing a garment similar to a dressing gown. The young woman on the right is from the Kustanay district

PLATE 3   These are all costumes from Estonia. The man in the traditional festive costume is from Setu. The shirt is in a typical Russian cut with the fastening on the left side. This is worn over striped linen trousers. The three-quarter length light coloured coat is decorated around the collar and down the front edges. The stockings have an ornamental design and the peasant shoes are made in a soft leather. The young girl in the centre is in a traditional costume of the Muhu district. The high collared shirt is decorated with cross stitch embroidery, crocheted lace and ribbons. The skirt is striped and ornamented with a floral pattern, as is the apron and small hat. The stockings and slippers are embroidered with floral motifs. The woman on the right is wearing the traditional costume of the Kihnu district. A high conical coif embroidered in brocade ribbon and lace covers her head. The short blouse is also profusely decorated. The skirt is striped and the apron is made in a patterned cotton print. The white socks have patterned tops and the shoes are made of sealskin. In the centre is a headdress worn in Vormsi Island by a bride. The high crowned hat is made of velvet and decorated with beads and flowers with decorated streamers hanging down the back

PLATE 4 *The young woman on the right is from the Ukraine. The woollen skirt is worn over a white petticoat. The apron is decorated. The long-sleeved white blouse is decorated in a floral pattern. The sleeveless jacket, usually in green, fastens on the left side. The edge of the jacket is trimmed with a band of braid. The headdress is made of a floral design and has hanging ribbons. Several rows of beads are also worn, and high red leather boots complete the outfit.*

The centre figure is of a man's costume of Syrjane from the district between Meses and Wytschegda. The loose thigh length shirt in blue checked pattern fastens on the right side with a short slit. The long narrow woollen girdle has fringed ends. The trousers are tucked into thick woollen socks and the shoes are of felt. The figure on the right is from the Oryel province and is dressed in the traditional costume of the early twentieth century. The dress is known as a sarafan and is a sleeveless garment hanging from shoulder straps. The headdress, usually the most elaborate and expensive part of the costume, known as a soroka, completely hides the hair. The background figure is of a woman from Byleorussia, from Povitye in the Kobrin district, who is wearing a traditional matchmaker's dress

PLATE 5   The centre figure is of a Turkmenian in a three-quarter length wrap-over gown or khalet in a striped material. At the back of the head he wears a velvet embroidered skull cap. He is playing the popular three stringed instrument, the balalaika. He is surrounded by children dressed in various traditional costumes from the past to the present day. The girls from Uzbekistan, on the left is in her eastern influenced costume, designed in a multi-coloured pattern. White trousers, tight at the ankles, are worn under the dress. A close fitting velvet embroidered cap or tyubeteika is worn towards the back of the head. A close-fitting velvet waistcoat is also worn on festive occasions. The girl showing her back is in a traditional costume from the Berezniki, Zhitkovichi district of Byelorussia. In the foreground a young girl is dressed in an older type dress with the skirt gathered and sewn onto the bodice. The hair is plaited and entwined with ribbon. She is from Vormsi in Estonia. The girl in the centre, dressed in a jacket, skirt and apron, is from Kotchino in the Mosty district of Byelorussia. On the right a young girl is in the costume of the youth organisation, a black skirt or tunic with the red pioneer scarf. In the background the boy is in the costume of northern Moldavia, with a fur hat and a sheepskin coat

PLATE 6 *On the* left *is an old Latvian costume worn only in the remoter areas. The loose cloak is fastened with a large metal brooch, one of the most distinctive features. The central figure is dressed in a mid-nineteenth century fashion from the Tambov district of the RSFSR. The red top is decorated in wide stripes of varying colours and designs. The back of the headdress is heavily fringed with beaded ends. The woman on the* right, *from the Voronezh province of the RSFSR, is wearing an early twentieth century dress*

PLATE 7 A festive costume from Turkmenistan is seen on the right. The dress is fairly tight fitting with embroidery at the seams and open edges. The looser fitting coat, matching and worn over the dress, is also embroidered or can be studded with metal discs. The round hat has a domed top with a metal point. The soft shoes are slightly turned up at the toes and have small heels. The woman on the extreme left, also from Turkmenistan, is with a small boy. They are wearing quilted coats, due to the extreme cold weather. They come from the high bleak Pamir mountains. In the centre the nomad from Azabaijan in the southern Caucasus is a Tatar. The Turkoman in the front, lower right, is wearing a karkul hat made of fur

PLATE 8 Three young people from Georgia. The Georgians are noted for their wine making and are seen here sampling some of it. The man on the left is wearing an embroidered shirt, whilst the one on the right is in a traditional Cossack uniform. The girl is in a flowing costume. The skirt is long and full, whilst the bodice of the dress is tight fitting with a high neckline and long sleeves. A veil falls behind from the small pill-box hat. The hair is dressed in two long plaits that hang down the front

Young Yakut girl wearing a fur hat

An older type folk costume from the Ryazan region. Over the embroidered ponyova *is worn an apron and bib made of transverse bands of embroidery*

hair at the back, whilst a married woman had to cover hers completely.

Towards the south a checked *yora* or skirt made of handwoven woollen cloth is worn with a long chemise or tunic called a *ponyova*, a sleeveless jacket and a headdress. The headdress consists of several parts with bead fastening at the back and fluff-ball decorations made of goosedown and beads.

In north-west Russia the quilted jackets are usually of brocade lined in a coarse linen and calico with a pleated basque at the back. The jackets are fastened with hooks and eyes and bands at the waist for adjustment gave a better fit.

Detachable brocade sleeves may be worn over those of the chemise and held in place with bands tied around the body. They are often worn instead of a short jacket beneath the sarafan and korotenka. Sometimes instead of being held on by bands, the sleeves are sewn on to the calico bodice that is not seen.

Kabardino is one of the autonomous replublics on the Caucasus mountains on the northern slopes, to the southern part of European Russia. The Adgei of this district are mainly horsemen and soldiers. Their embroidered garments often have distinctive crescent shapes in the design.

Women's costume consists of a blue or crimson velvet overdress. The flared panelled skirt and the long tight sleeves, with open sleeves attached, is reminiscent of a medieval western dress with the hanging sham sleeves. The dress worn beneath this has a bodice decorated with gold tassels. The front opening and collar are decorated with gold braid. The cap worn beneath a white veil is also embroidered in gold thread. Fez shaped caps are also worn.

The belts are generally of gold with large buckles, to which young girls have small bells attached. Footwear consists of either soft flat leather boots or high-heeled embroidered mules.

The men wear long high-necked belted tunics over wide trousers which they tuck into soft leather boots. The horsemen also wear dark felt overcoats, called *cherkeska*, each side of the chest being decorated with twisted cords, and around the waist from a narrow belt hangs the holster and dagger sheath made of gold.

The Caucasus area, bounded on the west by the Black Sea, and the Caspian Sea on the east, is the traditional land boundary between Asia Minor and the European Russia. The costumes, worn mainly by the dancers, are made in soft materials in subtle shades, showing Asian influence. Long full skirts are worn over equally long petticoats. The tops of the dresses are well fitting with a high neckline and the sleeves are long and tight. Dark coloured velvet jackets embroidered with gold are also worn. These have wide elbow-length sleeves revealing the sleeves of the gown beneath. Headwear is a silver band or velvet pill box hat, often decorated with coins, covered with a long white veil. The hair, in two plaits, is worn to the front.

Outside their tight fitting black trousers, the men wear a white shirt with long tight sleeves and a banded neckline, and have a cord around the waist of the shirt. A knee-length Cossack style coat has narrow pockets, the long sleeves completely covering the hands. These could be rolled back to reveal the shirt sleeves. Astrakhan hats are popular.

In the north-east Caucasus, in the province of Kalmyk, garments are often made of Chinese silk trimmed with tablet-woven silver braid. A gusset is inserted under the sleeves to which the garment is gathered. Towards the north, the kaftans are of quilted silks lined with colourful calico and black facings. Silver breast ornamentation is sewn on the leather bands.

Shot silk is in common use in the Caucasus. Many of the chemises are made of this material. In the Nakha area the Tatar women have the low front necklines decorated with ribbon and hanging coins. In the south-east the women usually encase their hair in calico or silk sheaths tied at the nape of the neck, and reaching up to the forehead.

The Avar women of the eastern Caucasus wear kaftans trimmed on the front edge with enamelled toggles, braid and gold cord being sewn on to the open edges.

These kaftans are also worn over a *beshmet* or *arkhaluk* which is a dress coat made of a quilted fabric with the front edges in a contrasting colour. The long sleeves are cut in a decorative design at the wrists.

In the south-eastern part of Daghestan, by the Caspian Sea, overgarments worn by Lezghin men are of a coarse dark blue woollen material made in a Persian style. The sleeves, left open at the lower side, caught at the wrists, are usually tied behind, or just left hanging. Trimming usually consists of gold braid, and the lining is a colourful calico. Instead of the usual cartridge casings on the chest, Lezghins would wear leather cartridge bags hanging from the shoulder. The full trousers are of coarse, smooth material, with a cord tied around the waist. The lamb-skin caps called *papakha* are widely worn. The leather boots have iron reinforcements with metal under the heels, the raised toes are also reinforced with iron.

Lady from the Kiev region wearing a hat decorated profusely with flowers and a green hip-length sleeveless jacket. The red skirt is embroidered

Woman from Ryazan wearing a festive headwear with a veil hanging at the back

Woman from Orel near the Tula district. The traditional apron with sleeves is profusely decorated with appliquéd bands of braid and calico with coloured stitching in between. The headdress is worn with a scarf that tied under the chin

Young Russian bride holding a candle symbolising Christ in the Orthodox ceremony

Kazan and Arsk, in the Tatar autonomous republic, in the eastern part of European Russia, are famous for their traditional shoes and boots. These are still made from small pieces of leather sewn together by hand. The boots, known as *ichigi*, are traditionally red or green. The toecaps and tops are ornamented with coloured pieces of leather in the shapes of unicorns, hearts, grape leaves or tulips.

To the north, in the Tatar province, the Chuvash women of Finnic descent wear colourful chemises that are belted. Their hoods are embroidered in bright colours and have coin covered strips hanging from them. A headscarf or *tastar* is wound around the head. In the eighteenth century crescent shaped hats were worn.

A typical Tatar coarse linen shirt is trimmed in brown wool sewn with blue cotton thread. The back resembles the shirts worn by the Caucasian Cherkess with a swallow-tail piece at the base. The front, however, is more in the style of seventeenth century Turkish designs with the decorative front edge running diagonally down the left, fastened with buttons and cords.

Towards the south-east in the autonomous republic of Chuvash, the men's shirts have calico gussets at the sides, similar to Persian or Indian fashions. The women's tops are similar to the men's shirts, but slightly more flared. The appliqué and embroidery are reminiscent of Oriental and Byzantine designs.

The festive dress of a Kazan woman is made of a stiff brocade. The dress is cut in an Oriental style with very long, wide sleeves. The base is decorated with a ruched gold braid and the collar fringed.

Many costumes in the Ryazan and Tula districts on the west are unique to these areas. In the districts south of Moscow women wear handwoven skirts with straight tunics, often with long waistcoats. Sarafans, with the bodice attached and buttoning down the front, are traditionally black or red for brides. Most of the costumes are woven in bright patterns – red being the dominant colour – aprons and sleeves are embroidered, and tunics and coats are decorated with braid – the whole effect being dramatic. Stiffened headdresses are worn over red scarves with a veil at the back. The headdress could be made of red felt sewn over a framework to stiffen it and be embroidered with gold thread and beads. Many headresses also have ruffles at the top, or multi-coloured pompons at the sides.

In summer hardly any footwear is worn, but during the extreme cold of winter, high thick felt boots are more practical.

In the province of Tula, the women wear a linen dress with a square embroidered neckline. The skirt is made up of appliquéd bands of red calico with decorative stitching between.

In the Smolensk province, to the west, the designs are of Slav origin. The chemise, known as a *rubakha*, is made in two parts, the lower half, is as usual, in a coarser linen. The long, wide sleeves are gathered to the neck and at the wrists. On the shoulders and on top of the sleeves they wear red calico bands trimmed with white zigzag braid and embroidery.

To the east, in the province of Ulyanovsk, the basic costume of Mordvin women – Finnic people of medium stature – is a belted chemise embroidered in a reddish brown and dark blue, worn over linen trousers. A linen apron trimmed in colourful bands of material and crochet work is worn with black and bead decorated side pieces beside which are red cloth-covered leather flaps, also decorated with beads and coins. A wide necklace of coloured beads is also worn. The headdress is a kind of Grenadier's bearskin over a silk kerchief hanging behind. Boots are also worn.

In the north, the autonomous republic of Udmurt, the Votyak women's overgarments have a slit in the upper part of the sleeves, through which the arms can pass, leaving the remainder hanging. The headdress is of a birch bark frame covered in a red material and trimmed with coins and tassels.

In the Vyatka area, the Cheremis, also Finnic people, wear a belted chemise similar to that of the Chuvash, decorated with bands of red calico appliqué. The leather neck ornaments are trimmed with silver coins and other trinkets. Linen trousers are wound round with dark woollen bands, and fibre shoes are worn. A coarse linen bonnet with embroidered edges has an oblong board-like ornament attached over the forehead.

A part of the older Cheremis costume which was replaced by a more general Russian one, is a 'Sunday' coat. This is made of coarse linen trimmed with red calico bands sewn with blue thread. Embroidered braid is used down the centre front and edges, and horizontal bands of wool cord are stitched across the front. A stylised Asian design in the form of a diagonal neckerchief is appliquéd on the chest, neck and over the shoulders. The extra-long sleeves are also characteristic of Asian apparel.

In the central eastern Russia, the chemise of the Votyak women is made of coarse linen, the upper part of the sleeves are decorated with red and brown embroidery with appliquéd

A woman in nineteenth century traditional costume, an Ersa-Mordavian from Arsatov in the province of Simbirsk. The belted linen chemise is embroidered, mainly in reddish brown and dark blue. The linen apron is trimmed with colourful fabric and crochet work. On her hips she has two bulging pieces made of black wool yarn and glass beads. She is also wearing a necklace of glass beads. The headdress is a kind of Grenadier cap worn over a silk kerchief. Under the chemise the woman wears linen trousers and accordion boots

Woman's boot worn with a festive costume from the Tula province ▶

calico bands. The rectangular side sections are box-pleated and sewn at the underarm. Over the chemise, cloth or linen garments with slit sleeves are worn.

In the Province of Penza, north of Moscow, the Mordvin women wear simple linen aprons over a belted chemise, with tiers of colourful striped pieces of material over the hips and back. Necklaces are usually chains of brass, coins and beads. The headdress is a wide cap stiffened at the top and covered in red cloth, trimmed with braid, ribbons, cords and silk rosettes. The long linen trousers, stockings and the accordion boots are barely visible under the long chemise.

In the Kaluga area to the south west of Moscow, the sleeves and shoulders of the chemise are usually in red calico, the upper part is of a fine linen gathered at the neck and joined to a narrow pink calico collar. The hem of the chemise is embroidered. The sarafan in this region is more like a sleeveless bodice joined to a gathered skirt.

From the sixteenth century onwards bright and colourful garments have become very popular in Russia, some with large figured designs. Outer garments that have been designed to be slipped into, are fastened in front and replace the shirt-like attire that is pulled over the head.

The folk costume worn by the Zyrians – Finnic people of stong and graceful build – consists of a shirt of coarse linen printed with a blue and white design, with a slit at the side; trousers of a thick felt-like wool in a dark colour, tucked into thick woollen socks, and felt shoes which have a loop at the back to hold the cord that ties around the ankles. Around the waist is bound a colourful woollen fringed belt. A round felt hat with a dark band is also worn.

Peasant woman from the Kaluga district wearing a linen chemise with calico sleeves and neck ruffle. The apron is richly embroidered and has an appliqué band at the base. The bast shoes and linen or wool bands are held on by thonging

◄ *Yakut woman in a fur with traditional beadwork ornamentation*

A Zyrian felt shoe

Hat of a Zyrian man from north west Russia, made of a light coloured felt and trimmed with black around the rim and with a black hatband

Festive clothes from the Tula province. The polushubok or outer garment was used as a blanket on overnight journeys in olden times

On the left is a peasant woman in a winter fur coat from Kiev. The girl in the centre, from the district of Vinnitsa in the Ukraine, is in a festive costume, whilst the man from the Zakarpahian is in summer dress

Woman's boot from the Tula ▶ province

Child's shoes from northern Russia

Festive wedding headdress of a young girl of the Vologda province, late nineteenth century

*Woman from the Kiev district
wearing a red satin coatee with gold,
red and green appliquéd embroidery*

*Animal breeder in the Kosh-Agach
region of Siberia wearing a fur hat
and coat*

*A young Samoyede from the Arctic Siberian area
using the reindeer as a means of transport. In the
foreground, holding his dog on a chain, is a man
from Kamchatka in the RSFSR, and to the right a
Udegets fur hunter and trapper from the Khabarovsk
in the RSFSR, the gateway to the Soviet Far East.
All these are of Mongoloid appearance*

Late nineteenth, early twentieth century clothes from the Arkhangel province. The tall stiff hat is lined in red and is of gold with a deep lace decoration. The white blouse is worn beneath a purple sarafan, and an orange scarf forms a type of collar. The shoes and boots are of a typical design

Girl in a rural dancing costume, from the Tuva ASSR

Child's soft boots from northern Russia

Handwoven straight tunic worn in a bright pattern from the Ryazan district

Votyak woman from the Glasgov district in the province of Vyatka. Her costume has a slit in the upper sleeve through which the arms can be passed, leaving the sleeve to hang. The headdress, an aishun, *has a supporting birch bark frame*

Typical Volga-Finn from the Pensa district. Over her belted chemise the woman wears a simple linen apron and decorative leather strips wtih glass beads. Over the back and hips there are tiers of coloured striped cloth. Other Mordvin women have tassel-like masses or braided pieces instead. A necklace consists of coins, brass chains and glass beads over which is worn another glass bead necklace with a cross hanging from it. A wide stiffened cap called a kapshav *is also worn. The chemise is worn over long*

linen trousers, linen stockings and accordion boots. Top centre shows the detail of the back of the headdress that consists of an oblong piece of card covered with red cloth or calico and trimmed with braid, ribbons and silk rosettes. The leather strip that hangs down is decorated with brass coins and the ends with an ornamental part made of shells, glass beads and chains with coins at the base. The detail beneath shows the front view with the cord and ribbon trim of the same headwear

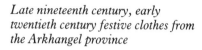

Late nineteenth century, early twentieth century festive clothes from the Arkhangel province

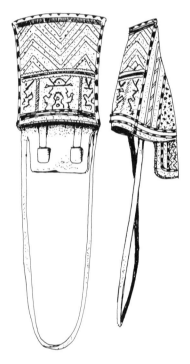

Front and side view of a cap, known as a pango, *from the Mordvinian ASSR in the RSFSR of a Volga-Finn. The front rounded part of the hat is made of birch bark covered with red cloth and trimmed with embroidery and glass beads. The back is stiffened with two flat wooden slat*

Nineteenth century Ryazan sarafan over a woman's dress, in red, with black appliqué and white embroidery

Mid nineteenth century festival clothes from the Tula province, front and back view. The headdress in the form of a rosette is matched by the smaller rosettes at the back of the skirt. They are in rings of varying colours, from the basic red with blue, yellow green and orange, and matching streamers. To the headdresses are attached white pompons on either side as well as the embroidered red streamers

Chuvash woman in a colourfully stitched belted chemise. A scarf or tastar is wound around the head

From the Arkhangel district, the detached sleeves just join at the back and are held in place with bands tied around the body. They are worn under the sarafan and korotenka instead of a short jacket

Nineteenth century short jackets known as rukhava, worn in the Arkhangel province of the RSFSR

Natiai woman of the Khabarovsk region, towards China, in a traditional dress

Buryat woman native to Siberia. Earring, bead necklaces and flat silver ornaments are worn. The wealthier of the tribe wore very elaborate costumes

Man from the Vologda province in a asyami or loose coat with a belt. He is holding an astrakhan cap in his hand and wearing high boots

The chemise is embroidered on the ▶ eams and edges, and over this is worn a sleeveless belted red calico smock with a green trimming. The legs are covered with coarse linen bands and the shoes are made of bast

Handwoven girl's coat of the mid-nineteenth century from the Orel province. It is close fitting at the waist, the collar lined with calico. It is dark brown with red cord and embroidered edgings and front. This style was popular throughout Russia until the 1920s, and could also be worn by men

Costume of a Chermis woman

Early twentieth century winter clothing of a man from Buryato-Mongolia

Shaman priest from Siberia in ceremonial attire holding a type of tambourine, and hanging from his back, a selection of bells, nails, coins and other oddments

This lady from RSFSR is seen wearing a late eighteenth century costume, consisting of a brocade skirt starting at the hips, and a Tatar jacket with a basque

45

THE CAUCASUS

Armenian peasant girl wearing her native costume including the leather shoes with the toes pointing upwards. She is wearing ornate jewellery and her headwear is also bejewelled

ARMENIA

Armenia, with Azerbaijan and Georgia form Transcaucasia, each republic with its own history and ancient culture, and traditional costumes which survive today. Armenia is the smallest of the Soviet Republics and has had a tragic and turbulent history. It is the oldest Christian nation. Mount Ararat can be seen from the capital city of Yerevan. The Armenians are a hardy race, tall and dark. The women are famous for their hand embroidery.

In the south Caucasian area of Leninaken, the traditional dress of the Yezidi women consists of red velvet unlined garments with a velvet apron, lined with printed calico. The hem of the dress and the edges of the aprons being trimmed with a zigzag design. An ornate *plastron* made of pieces of coloured silk with glass beads and buttons is tied to the chest with strings around the neck and waist. High soft leather inner boots are worn over ankle-length leather boots decorated with appliqué and impressed designs.

The kaftans worn by Armenian women from Akhaltsikh are of a coarse striped silk with thin gold braid around the neckline. The front is edged with silk covered buttons. The sleeves are further lengthened with false sleeves in a contrasting colour to imitate an undergarment. These are cut in a zigzag and decorated with gold braid. The caps have long silk tassels.

In Akhaltsikh the women wear short silk damask jackets edged with gold cord, the sleeves ending in a point. The trousers are of a coarser silk, and the leather slippers, with long toes pointing upwards, are embroidered in red.

The undergarments, made of oriental taffeta silk with printed calico insets, are covered by an overgarment such as a dress, coat or kaftan. The neck edge is decorated with gold braid.

The leather slipper is covered with embroidered red cloth and a green inner sole – from Akhaltsikh

An inner boot made of very soft leather ▶

An ankle-length leather boot with cloth appliqué work and points, with lines pressed into the leather

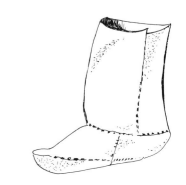

Woman from a far scattered tribe of Yezedi from Mount Ararat

A Kurd from the Yerevan area wears wide trousers elaborately trimmed with silk and gold cord and tied around the waist with a drawstring. The form of their sleeved waistcoats can be traced back to a kaftan in style and are almost always of a striped fabric, closing with small buttons at the neck. Braid is sometimes added down the front to give the impression of an ornate type of fastening.

AZERBAIJAN

Azerbaijan, a mountainous country, rich in oil, is bordered on the north by the RSFSR, on the southwest by Armenia and Georgia, south by Iran and on the east by the Caspian Sea.

The dry, sub-topical climate is characterised in central and eastern areas by mild winters and bright summers, and in the south east by humid sub-topical conditions.

After the Russian Revolution, Azerbaijan became the first Moslem Republic, Tatars with Turkish affinities and Turkish speaking, forming the majority of the population. They have influenced the Russian character by mingling their eastern blood with that of the Slavs, and by introducing Persian and Chinese culture, from which their costumes have been adapted. Characteristic of Azerbaijan, however, are the large bearskin hats worn by the men. They also have astrakhan collars to their coats.

The proud and ancient peoples of Azerbaijan's remoter areas retain many distinctive folk traditions.

Young woman from Azerbaijan in a festive costume. She wears her hair in two long plaits

Woman in a typical headdress

Typical costume of the Cossack type with a fur hat

47

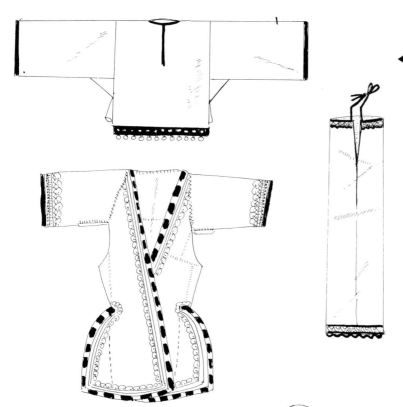

Chemise of a Tatar woman from Nukha in South East Caucasus. It is made of shot silk and trimmed with black ribbon and a row of hanging coins with gold plates at the base

The hair sheath of a Tatar woman. In south east Caucasus the hair is usually encased in a sheath made of calico or silk and trimmed at both ends with braid

Tatar woman's jacket from Shemakha in the south-east Caucasus. it is made of velvet and lined in silk, trimmed with lace work of Caucasian braid and fine gold braid

Typical Azabaijan woman's costume

Tatar man in a traditional flowing robes and a tall astrakhan hat

Man wearing the traditional astrakhan headwear

48

GEORGIA

Georgia is in the region that borders the east coast of the Black Sea, and is a land of scenic beauty, experiencing extreme ranges of temperature, from perpetual snow to sub-tropical heat, and its natural resources abound.

The Georgians belong to the Kartvelian group of Indo-Caucasians, one of the most ancient races in the world, and speak one of the oldest living languages. The Georgian love of finery can be seen in the bright colours of the materials and their picturesque clothing.

Decorative silver belts are worn by both men and women. Typical of Georgia, is an astrakhan cap, called a *papakh*, worn by the men. In winter a large, sleeveless semi-circular cloak made of thick felt from goats' or horses' hair, called a *bourka*, is worn, one end of which is flung over the left shoulder. Being waterproof, this cloak can also act as a warm blanket. The round neck opening is trimmed with braid and fastened with a cord. A long coat or jacket, called a *cherkeska*, made of a rough woollen material mainly in sombre colours with tablet-woven trimmings, is worn when it is not too cold. The skirt at the back of the coat is pleated to the upper part, and fitted at the waist. Cloth cartridge cases decorate the chest, and around the waist a narrow belt holds a dagger in front. Beneath the coat a cotton or linen tunic, loose trousers and leggings are worn.

The women wear similar jackets with skirts and bodices adorned with silver filigree chains and buckles. The most unusual part of their dress is a stiff velvet band worn around the head which holds a large white veil with two long false curls attached to the band. For wedding wear the veils are of fine lace. For mourning white veils are worn without decoration.

Typical Georgian man in his picturesque costume

Typical Georgian farm woman with a headscarf

Young Caucasian boy in a white parade costume with small dagger, cartridge cases, fittings and Caucasian trimmings in a replica of an adult Georgian Cossack

The man in the background, early twentieth century, is a Georgian peasant playing his bagpipe, one of the oldest forms of musical instruments. The young Caucasian girl of the early twentieth century is wearing a silk coat over loose trousers caught in at the ankles. On her head she wears a stiff scarlet velvet band ornamented with pearls and two long false plaits. The Georgian peasant, of the same period, is wearing gaily coloured baggy trousers

Georgian dancer with an astrakhan hat, high boots and the coat embellished with cartridge cases

50

Headwear of a Kazakh dancer

KAZAKHSTAN

Kazakhstan extends from the Caspain Sea on the south-west to China in the east. On the north and north-west it is bounded by the RSFSR, and on the south by Turkmenia, Uzbekistan and Kirghizia. Steppes and desert dominate the landscape and the climate is marked by extremes with hot summers and cold winters.

The native Kazakhs comprise less than 30% of the population and their strong Islamic tradition is tolerated.

The peasant women wear linen chemises, sarafans and aprons. The chemise – a long, loose type of blouse – has calico sleeves and a frilled collar, the embroidered edges of which are visible beneath the sarafan which is also decorated with a broad band of appliqué at the hem.

Young girls, generally, wear embroidered pill-box caps. For weddings, brides cover their heads with a red shawl, and once mothers they usually wear a white headdress and a white collar, also less ornamentation.

Men's folk costumes from the Mogilev area consists of linen trousers and a shirt, as well as a wrap-over coat with a stand-up collar, known as a *karakin*, in grey wool for winter and made of natural coloured linen for summer wear. The women may also wear a karakin with a woollen belt over the dress.

Both men and women wear *lapti*, which are shoes made of the inner bark of trees or from tree fibres. The woollen or linen bands wound around their feet and calves are held on by cord or thonging.

In east central Russia coarse felt-like woollen material is used for coats. The appliqué work, mainly on the yoke, is of red calico trimmed with glass beads, porcelain buttons and shells. The edges are trimmed with red wool.

The dress of the Bashkir women is influenced by Turkic designs, although there are also traces of Volga-Finnish influence. The main adornment of the dress is a *plastron*. The hats have long leather strips covered in shells, coins and glass beads hanging behind. Boots, usually high, in some areas they were of black leather, and in others, they made of a coarse cloth.

Musician from Kazakh

Young Kazakh girl in a festive headdress that is in the shape of a pill-box embroidered and topped with feathers

51

The overgarments of the Bashkirs are made from coarse natural coloured wool, with an inset into the sleeve seam.

For festive occasions the costume is of a dark grey with a double row of braid along the edges. The coat-like garment is lined in grey blue striped calico. This type of garment is also worn by men when it was usually in red or blue.

Special coats are made from the fur of the snow leopard and hats from the fur of the red fox.

A 1920s bridegroom's costume from the Semipalatinsk province of Kazakh SSR. The hat was decorated with woollen pompons, buttons and ribbon

Uzbek worker from central Asia. The headwear is reminiscent of Islamic styles

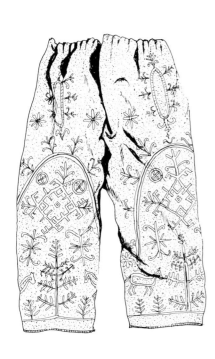

Uzbek girl wearing a gold embroidered cap, known as doppi, *over her black hair which is dressed in forty plaits. The cap is made in four sections*

UZBEKISTAN

Lady from Uzbek dressed in a mixture of modern and traditional clothing

An Uzbek man from Tashkent

Uzbekistan is a country of vast desert landscapes and fertile oases. It is bounded by Kazakhstan and Tadzhkstan on the east and Turkmenistan on the south-west. It is the most densely populated area of Central Asia, made up of some 60 different peoples, two-thirds of which are Uzbeks. When Bukhara and Khiva came under Soviet rule in 1925, the two states were linked together to form Uzbekistan. Bukhara lies in the heart of a vast desert region. As is the custom, the men wear a brightly coloured silk or cotton *khalet*, with a coloured kerchief tied around the waist, over a white shirt and dark trousers tucked into his boots. The trousers are often made of dyed sheepskin, lined with calico. He also wears a red and blue striped turban decorated with coloured stones.

In contrast the women have sombre attire, wearing trousers beneath their dark coloured dresses and tunics which have a white muslin inset at the top. The Dervish of Bukhara wear hats of dark fabric with a lamb-skin pompon, some being made in four sections, embroidered and edged with fur.

Striped kaftans are also worn with a silk sash around the waist. The loose trousers, tucked into leather boots, and a velvet skull cap, a *tyubeteika* – worn throughout Central Asia by both men and women – is embroidered or decorated with tassels and coloured stones.

In Samarkand the chemise is usually of a soft silk with the pattern achieved by a tie-dye method. Black braid is often used along the edges and neck openings.

The indigenous races of Central Asian republics is reflected in their Islamic mode of dress. The designs on the cotton materials are a mixture of multi-coloured patterns and stripes.

One of the most popular costumes of the Uzbek women is a calf-length dress with a turned-up collar and loose, wide wrist-length sleeves, over plain cotton trousers which blend in well with the patterned dress.

On festive occasions women wear brightly coloured silk dresses with a coloured or dazzling white shawl over their heads.

TURKMENISTAN

Shepherd from Bukhara wearing a white linen turban

Turkmenistan is the southermost Republic of the USSR, bordering Iran and Afghanistan, it lies in Central Asia, just south of the Steppes and is bleak desert, currently being reclaimed by irrigation. It has been inhabited from the tenth century by Turkic peoples of which the *Tekke* of *Teppe* are the most important.

The principal inhabitants of Soviet Turkmenistan which lies north of Afghanistan and India and to the south-east of the Caspian Sea, are called the Sarts, and they are the strictest Mahomedans in the world. Their ample white turbans and flowing robes are biblical in style.

Peculiar to Central Asia were the *batcha* or dancing boys chosen for their good feminine looks. They travelled with a manager from place to place in groups of about ten and were hired out to entertain people with their dancing. Their hair was worn long to give them a feminine appearance. They dressed in brightly coloured tunics and loose trousers with high leather boots. The small peaked caps fitted closely and were profusely embroidered in coloured silks.

The Turkmen, also important people of this area, are akin to the Bedouins in their way of life. They shave their heads so caps are always worn beneath their turbans. Beards are allowed to grow and may never be cut. Even babies have their hair shaven, the girls being allowed to grow theirs from the age of seven.

Unmarried girls wear no headdress indoors, allowing their thick straight black hair to hang down in several plaits.

The Sart women, the most secluded of their sex in the world, wear a thick black horse-hair veil and a grey garment with long tapering sleeves fastened together at the back.

They join their eyebrows with a black dye line, sometimes even extending it, on either side of the face, to the ears. The fingernails and palms of the hands are stained with henna.

Over their baggy cotton trousers and coarse shirt the men wear a wide-sleeved coat in a coloured material. Their boots are usually high heeled. A distinctive part of the Turkmen dress is the large shaggy black sheep's-wool cap, rather like a bearskin, and a gaudy scarlet sash around the waist.

Turkmenian dancers in the kaftan style festive costumes

54

A Turkmenian farmer in traditional large sheepskin hat

In spite of modernisation, the camel is still much respected in Turkmenistan. The female is a source of rich milk as well as of wool that can be used for fabrics, blankets and knitted garments.

The centuries' old custom of ornamenting the camel still exists. Traditionally the 'desert ship' is covered with a horse-hair rug, the head and neck decorated with many intertwined straps, beads, cords and tassels in a multitude of colours. A necklace consisting of copper bells is usually the finishing touch. The camel's attire can be as important to the Turkmen as their own dress.

Not as strict in their religion as the Sarts, they allow their women to go about unveiled. They adorn themselves with large and impressive jewellery such as heavy breast-plates and thumb rings. Their silver bracelets and anklets are so large that they cover most of their limbs. The silver amulets containing parts of the Koran are decorated with silver coins and ornaments.

The women wear colourful loose fitting kaftans with full trousers of a contrasting colour, ending in decorative bands. Their dresses are tight fitting, usually in dark red or orange. The seams of the front panel and the sides are embroidered in white. The neckline and centre openings are also decorated.

A loose three-quarter length coat of the same material and colour may be worn over the dress on formal occasions, the front edge, hem and sleeves being embroidered or decorated with metal discs. Cottons and heavy silks are worn in the summer, whilst woollen materials are needed in the winter.

Hair is worn in two plaits with a small round domed hat with a metal tip. Head-scarves and embroidered caps are also worn. Their low-heeled soft shoes have slightly turned-up toes.

The men's shirts are usually dark in colour, embroidered around the neck and opening on the right side. They are worn outside tight-fitting black or brown trousers with a brightly coloured sash around the waist. The trousers are tucked into high black boots.

In winter they wear a characteristic long-sleeved quilted coat, usually tied around the waist with a narrow band. Extremely large white or brown sheepskin hats may also be worn with loose three-quarter length striped coat.

A Sart bride with a thick horsehair veil and a long grey garment covering her from head to foot

A girl in a Turkmenian high headdress richly embroidered, with a scarf over it, worn for festive occasions

To the back right is a Kirghiz woman from the Pamir mountains, dressed in a long loose quilted coat and heavy walking boots. The horseman in the centre, also from the Pamir is playing a game of baigu, *a mixture of polo and rugby, using the body of a decapitated goat as a ball. The Sarikoli is wearing an extremely long-sleeved rose coloured coat. He uses the sleeves for his dance as much as his bare feet. Seated in the foreground is a Turkmenian camel-driver, resting during his journey across the Kara-Kum desert in Central Asia. He is wearing a* karkul *hat*

Young Sart girl in a padded coat and long padded trousers

A Sart lady with a thick horsehair veil thrown back

A nomadic rider on his wiry horse from Khiva, mainly desert land. He is wearing a turban headdress. On the left the Kirghiz woman is also a nomad wearing a striped kaftan. The dancing boy from Khiva is dancing a dance from which the Russian ballet had its origin. Unlike the Uzbeks or Turkmen, the Sart is one of the most stable of races in this nomadic area. This man is wearing a loose coat held together with a sash and baggy trousers tucked into high boots

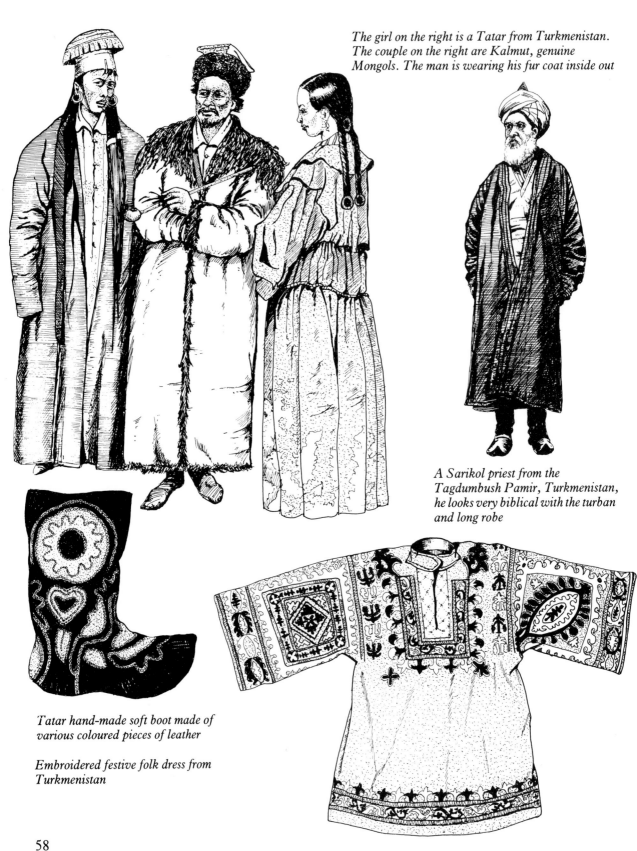

The girl on the right is a Tatar from Turkmenistan.
The couple on the right are Kalmut, genuine
Mongols. The man is wearing his fur coat inside out

A Sarikol priest from the
Tagdumbush Pamir, Turkmenistan,
he looks very biblical with the turban
and long robe

Tatar hand-made soft boot made of
various coloured pieces of leather

Embroidered festive folk dress from
Turkmenistan

KIRGHIZIA

Typical Kirghiz woman

Kirghizia is a mountainous country with cold winters and hot dry summers; shortage of water has caused many hardships to the peoples. It is bounded on the north by Kazakhstan, on the west by Uzbekistan and on the south and south west by Tadzhikistan.

The Kirghizians, former nomads whose ancient and colourful traditions date back to the beginning of recorded history, make up about one-third of the population. Kirghizia, however, is now the home of some 80 nationalities.

The Kirghiz are sub-divided into the Kazakhs and the Kara-Kirghiz. The Kazakhs live in the lowlands, whilst the Kara-Kirghiz are the highlanders. Similar costume is worn by both Kazakh men and women, consisting of a khalet which is a long flowing robe of cotton, silk or velvet, fastened with a leather girdle which, for the men, holds a knife, tobacco pouch and other trinkets.

Baggy cloth or silk trousers are worn over the khalet, high black or red leather boots and round felt printed caps complete the costume.

A shepherd from Kirghizia wearing a traditional hat

Kirghiz woman with coin and metal decorations

TADZHIKISTAN

The Soviet Socialist Republic of Tadzhikistan is a mountainous country with a dense network of rivers, and has a climate of extreme temperatures. It is in west central Asia, bounded on the north and west by Uzbekistan and on the north-east by Kirghizia. It was acquired as part of Turkistan in 1895 and formed parts of Bukhara and Turkistan when it became a Constituent Republic in 1929. Although multinational indigenous peoples, the Tadzhiks, of Iranian origin, comprise over half the population.

Woman's national headdress from the northern regions of Tadzhikstan

The Tadzhiks are of the Muslim faith. The women wear veils over their headdress and the men shave their heads but do not allow their beards to grow long. The dress is simple, the principal garment being the *khalet*, worn with a white linen turban. It is a land of ancient culture and many of the traditions and customs are still practised today.

The long copper trumpets were only used on important occasions and were about 2.5 metres long, making a noise like a bellowing bull. They were used by the Tadzhiks or Sarts who wore striped kaftans with a sash around the waist, white shirts were worn beneath the coats and the headwear was of Turkish style

GLOSSARY OF COSTUME TERMS

Young Tadzhik girl dancing in a folk costume of Persian style

Woman's festive namitka, from Tyshkovichi in the Ivanovo district Byelorussia

Aishun	A headress with a supporting birch bark frame
Asyami	A loose coat with a belt
Beshmet or arkhaluk	A quilted dress coat with front edges of a contrasting colour
Bourka	A large waterproof semi-circular cloak of felt from goat or horse hair
Calpac	A tall hat of white felt decorated with beads
Chemise	A long loose type of smock
Cherkeska	A dark felt overcoat with a row of cartridge pockets either side of the chest
Chereviki	Shoes made of coloured pieces of leather
Doppi	An embroidered gold cap
Fata or dymka	Long, wide muslin veil
Ichigi	Red or green boots with toecaps and tops ornamented with coloured pieces of leather
Kapshav	A stiff cap
Karuna	A crown-like headdress
Karakin	A wrap-over coat with a stand-up collar made in grey wool for winter and natural coloured linen for summer
Khalet	A long flowing coat dyed in bright colours
Kichka	A horned headdress
Korotenka or paneka	A short dress similar to a sarafan
Khoty	Leather shoes trimmed with nails
Klumpès	Wooden shoes with carved or painted ornamentation
Kokoshnik	A headdress with a large bow at the back profusely decorated with beads and semi-precious stones
Lapti	Shoes made from birch bark or lime tree fibre
Namitka or nuometas	Lengths of white linen wound around the head and neck, the ends hanging loose down the back or over the shoulders

Naverschnik	An ancient type of tunic often in black worn as an overgarment
Obory	Thonging or strings wound around the legs to keep the shoes on
Paneka or korotenka	Short dress similar in style to a sarafan
Pango	A cap, the front part of which is made of birch bark covered with red cloth and trimmed with embroidery. The back is stiffened with two flat wooden slats
Pastali	Hide sandals
Papakh	An astrakhan cap
Plakha	An apron covering both front and back woven in brightly coloured horizontal stripes
Plastron	The ornamental front to the bodice of a woman's dress
Pokosnitsa	A blouse worn by young girls
Polushubok	A cloak which can be used as a blanket on overnight journeys
Ponyova	A long shirt or tunic
Rubakha	A chemise made in two parts: the lower half in a coarser fabric than the top half
Rukhava	A short nineteenth century jacket
Sarafan	Either a skirt or combined skirt and bodice buttoned in front. With the former a separate sleeveless bodice would be worn
Shugais	A quilted or padded jacket
Simtakvaldis	A knee-length coat pleated from the bust down
Soroka	A complicated headdress trimmed in multi-coloured glass beads, gold thread, feathers and fringes
Svita	A type of overcoat of white, grey or brown homespun cloth, tight at waist and trimmed with coloured cords
Tastar	A headscarf
Tyubeteika	A velvet, embroidered cap decorated with tassels and coloured stones
Valenki	Felt boot worn in winter
Vorotushka	A shirt-blouse of fine linen with red
Yora	A skirt of handwoven woollen cloth

A plastron *worn over a woman's costume, made of cloth and silk and decorated with glass beads and buttons*

Woman's headwear – a soroka *worn in the late nineteenth century. It is red with heavy gold embroidery in the front and embellished with red and black tassels. From the Orel province, RSFSR*

BIBLIOGRAPHY

BRUHN, W, and TILKE, M, *Pictorial History of Costume*, Zwemmer 1955

FOX, LILLA M, *Folk Costumes from Eastern Europe*, Chatto and Windus 1977

GILBERT, J, *National Costumes of the World*, Hamlyn 1972

HAMMERTON, J A, *Lands and Peoples*, Almagamated Press

HAMMERTON, J A, *Peoples of all Nations*, Amalgamated Press 1922-1924

HARROLD, R and LEGG, P, *Folk Costumes of the World*, Blandford 1978

HEWITT, P, *Looking at Russia*, A & C Black 1977

KAARMA, M, SUMERA, M, & VOOLMAA, A, *Estonian Folk Costumes* Tallinn 'Eesti Raamat' 1981

LIVSCHITS, M Y and ZYERINA, A M, *National Costume of Moldavia*, State House, Kartya, Moldavia, Kizhnev 1960

MANN, KATHLEEN, *Peasant Costume in Europe*, A & C Black 1950

ROMANYUK, M, *Byelorussian National Dress*, Minck 1981

SNOWDEN, J, *The Folk Dress of Europe*, Mills and Boon 1979

STASE, BERNITIENE, *Women's Folk Costume of Lithuania*, Mintis, Vilnius 1974

TILKE, M, *Costume Patterns and Designs*, Zwemmer 1956

TILKE, M, *Folk Costume*, Zwemmer 1978

TURNER-WILCOX, R, *Folk and Festival Costumes of the World*, Batsford 1965

Latvia Nineteenth to Twentieth Century, Ethnographic Museum 1981

Russian Folk Clothing, State Ethnographical Museum of the People of the USSR, Khudozhnik 1984

Ukranian Folk Art, State House of Fine Arts, Music and Literature, Kiev 1961

Early twentieth century male costume from the Olonets province. The loose fitting white shirt is embroidered at the hem and sleeve edges in red and the front side opening edged with red braid. Around the waist the red sash ends with tassels. The shoes are made of plaited straw and fastened with thonging

INDEX